MW00892576

# THE FARM CHICKEN'S NEW SHOES

Written by
Mariah Nienhuis

Illustrated by
Logan Dais

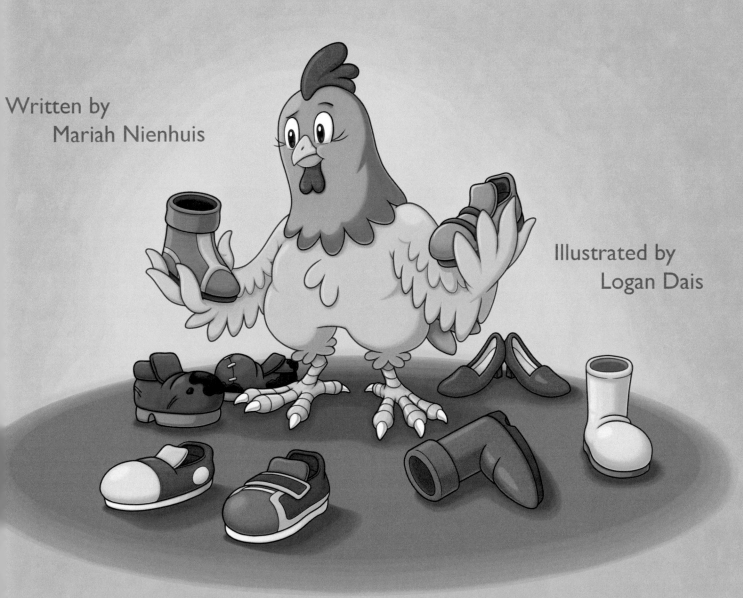

# This book is dedicated to:

First, to my husband and children, my biggest why. And also, to my parents as an appreciation to raising me to know that I can do anything I put my mind to as long as God is with me.

- M.N.

Philippians 4:13

I'm Edna, and do you want to know my biggest pet peeve? No one sells a shoe that fits a chicken! Don't laugh, this is serious!

Sure, it might seem unnecessary to YOU! But when I find myself walking to town, getting chased by a Billy goat, or running after a bus I missed, it's anything but funny.

The only shoes I could find did not fit my three and a half toes. They were crammed together and, boy, did I walk and run funny!

After I searched high and low, do you know what I decided to do? Did I give up? Certainly not! I decided to go shopping.

After a delicious lunch of corn and chicken feed, I got ready to wobble to town!

I laid an egg, took a dust bath, and brushed my feathers. I wanted to look nice!

I had to put on my miserable shoes.

In town I checked out all the stores.

I tried different styles, and different sizes.
The bigger sizes were clumsy.
The heels were horrible.
There were some really nice boots…

…and I almost settled with them, but I couldn't even pull them on without falling to the floor! Ugh!

I even found shoes that fit horses, but nothing for chickens. Really? Then, I looked across the road and saw it...a shoemaker's store! I hurried inside.

"Can I help you?" the shoemaker asked kindly.

"Yes, I hope so."

The shoemaker sat back from what he was doing and thought for a bit. He finally responded, "You know, let's see what we can do."

He sketched, measured, and talked about style. "I need something nice for town-- a shoe that I can run, jump, and scratch around the farm in," I said eagerly.

Mr. Fredrickson showed me the shoe design.
"How about bows instead of buckles?" I suggested.
He tried again.
"That's it!" I clapped.

"They should be ready in two weeks!" Mr. Fredrickson said.
Heading back to the farm, I was one excited hen!

2 WEEKS LATER...

Finally, the day came. This time as I was putting on my pesky shoes, I had high hopes that it would be the last time!

The shoemaker welcomed me with a smile. "You are going to love how your shoes came together!" He said joyfully. I couldn't wait to see them!

I waited for Mr. Fredrickson who had gone to the back of the store to get the finished shoes for me.

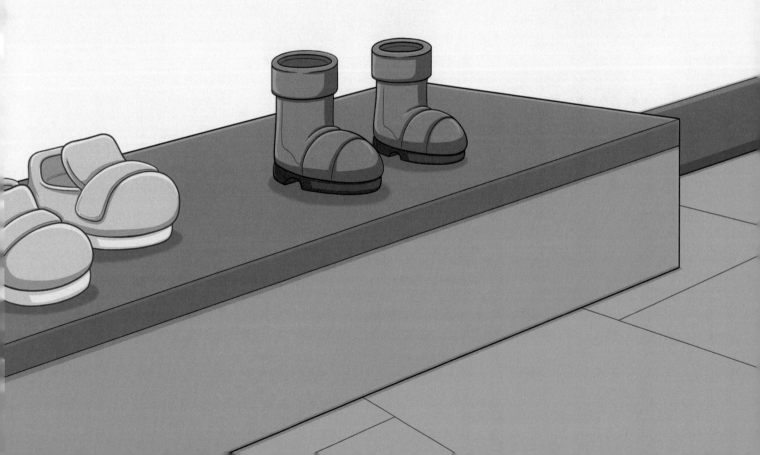

My new shoes! They looked stunning! A lovely red shoe, nicely stitched, comfortable, and perfectly practical! And best of all was the wonderful way the shoe curved in and out to match the shape of my chicken feet!

He set them down in front of me and I anxiously slipped them on. Oh, was I dreaming? They fit great! No more cramped toes for this hen!

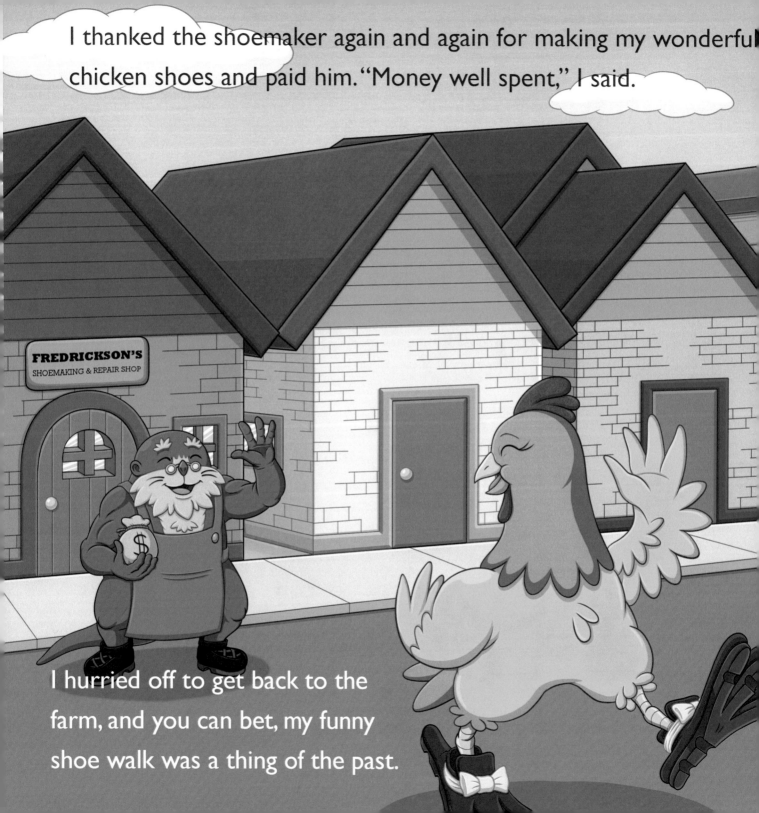

Mariah Nienhuis, Author

Hello! My name is Mariah, and this book captures my childhood imagination and literally puts it in book form. I have always loved chickens and farming intrigues me. The very idea came to me as a child… what kind of shoes could a chicken actually comfortably wear? Now fast forward and I have my very own flock of hens. I hope you find Edna the hen quirky and fun, and you are able to giggle along with her as she tries to find the perfect shoe. With a touch of life on the farm I hope this gives your little one a little taste of what a chicken's life is like on the farm.

Logan Dais, Illustrator

Hi there! My name is Logan. Growing up, I always enjoyed drawing pictures for the younger children at church and my neighborhood. I am now so thankful for the opportunity to illustrate this storybook.

Printed in the USA
CPSIA information can be obtained
at www.ICGtesting.com
LVRC081225281024
794902LV00009B/138

Made in the USA
Middletown, DE
02 June 2017